Nature Discoveries
with Uncle Mike

These [sailors] see the works of the LORD,
and his wonders in the deep. Psalm 107:24

Wonders in the
SEA

MIKE ATNIP

ISBN: 978-1-943929-69-6

Cover photo: © shutterstock.com

Printed in China

Published by:
TGS International
P.O. Box 355, Berlin, Ohio 44610 USA
Phone: 330-893-4828 | Fax: 330-893-2305 | www.tgsinternational.com

TGS001448

God has placed many wonders in
the deep waters of the oceans.
Let's go see what we can find.
Ready? Let's go!

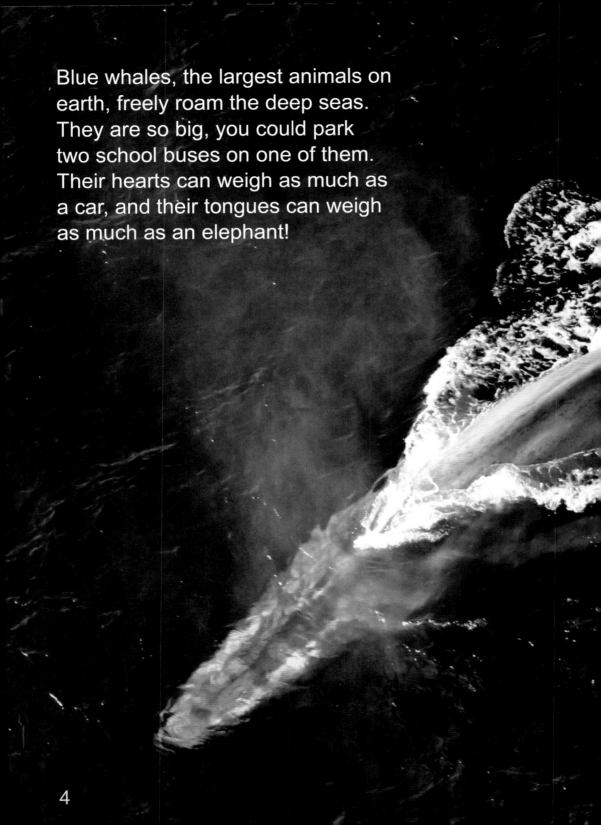

Blue whales, the largest animals on
earth, freely roam the deep seas.
They are so big, you could park
two school buses on one of them.
Their hearts can weigh as much as
a car, and their tongues can weigh
as much as an elephant!

The skull of this blue whale is nineteen feet long. Can you guess what blue whales eat? On the next page we will see a sample of their food.

Yes, this is whale food! This species of krill grows to a little over two inches long. The picture above is life size!

To get enough food to stay alive, blue whales must eat millions and millions of these small krill every day. They catch swarms of krill by opening their mouths and taking big gulps of water. The water is then filtered out, and the krill is swallowed.

Killer whales (also called orcas) have sharp teeth. Many eat large animals like seals and sea lions. They like to jump out of the water.

Although basking sharks have huge mouths, divers do not fear them because they eat only small animals like krill. They can filter over 8,000 gallons of water per minute!

What else, besides sharks and whales, do you expect to find in the ocean? Let's go see if we can find zebras, lions, whips, saws, trumpets, footballs, and much more. You don't think these are in the ocean? Well, let's go see.

We'll start with a whip. Here is a whipnose angler. This fish can live in water over half a mile deep. It puts the whip in front of it as a lure for smaller fish. When the small fish come to the lure, the angler quickly eats them.

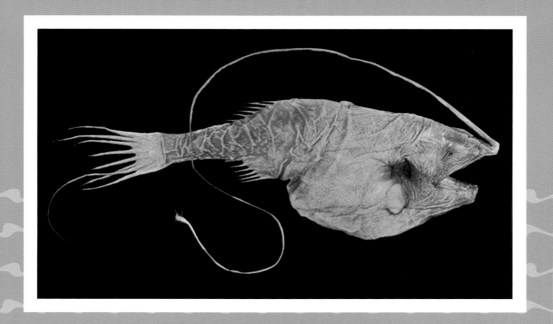

Would you care for an apple? This sea apple is not a fruit, though. It is an animal! It has little tube-like feet that it uses to walk along the ocean floor.

Does this look like a cucumber? The chocolate chip sea cucumber looks a bit like caramel candy dotted with chocolate. But like the sea apple, this is a living animal.

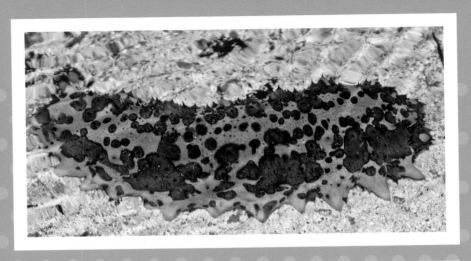

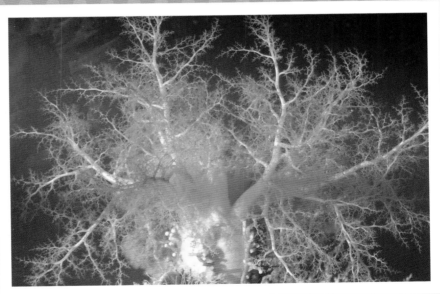

This is the mouth of another sea cucumber. The tentacles are used to draw food into its mouth.

How about
a trumpet in
the sea? This
trumpetfish
looks like a horn
of some kind.
Even its color
looks like brass.
Many times the
trumpetfish will
keep its body
straight up and
down while
swimming so
that it looks like
a weed.

Believe it or not, sponges are also animals. The yellow one is a tube sponge. The purple one is called a vase sponge. The red one is an encrusting sponge, and the gray one across the tube sponge is a rope sponge. It is almost impossible to kill these animals because they can grow back lost body parts. Also, if you cut a piece off of a sea sponge, the piece can grow into an entire new sponge.

The red lionfish does not roar like a lion, but it has poisonous spines on its back. Just like lions, they sometimes form small groups of a male and a few females. They fiercely defend their territory.

This crocodilefish is shaped like a crocodile.
It uses its camouflage to hide from smaller fish,
snatching them for a meal as they swim by.

Lions and crocodiles . . . and now zebras!
This zebra moray eel gets its name from its
zebra stripes. Eels look like they are half
snake and half fish. They like to live in holes
among the rocks on the ocean bottom.

17

That looks like a hedge trimmer! It is actually the "saw" of a sawfish. However, this fish does not saw wood. It uses the saw like a sword to kill other fish and like a shovel to dig into the muddy sea floor to find food.

The pink-winged flying fish can glide through the air with its large front fins spread out like bird wings. By flapping its tail really fast, the fish is lifted out of the water.

Sea turtles have flippers instead of feet. They cannot fly like a flying fish, but they are great swimmers. Sea turtles can grow as long as an adult human and weigh as much as five adults!

19

Do you know the name of this animal? It's a pot-bellied seahorse. You can see why it got the name "pot-bellied." And doesn't its head look like a horse's head? The seahorse uses its curly tail to hang on to things when it wants to stop and catch small animals to eat.

Would you expect to see a football in the ocean, perhaps floating on the waves? The football fish swims deep in the waters, sometimes over half a mile down. The strands on the top are used as a lure. In some football fish, bacteria that glow in the dark live in the lure, making the lure glow.

What would you name this fish if you could choose the name? It sort of looks like a dried-up apple, so how about the "dried apple fish"?

These sea spiders are not spiders, but you can see why people named them that way. Many sea spiders like to eat sea sponges. It's a good thing the sponge can regrow the parts the sea spider eats!

God has put lilies in the sea. No, they are not plants, but animals called sea lilies. If you look at this one, you will see that it is hanging on with what looks like wormy roots. These are not roots, but legs.

The sea lily uses its feathery arms to sweep food into its mouth, which is in the center of the "flower." It is so amazing what God has created!!

The red lily has a stem with a feathery head, but it is an animal, not a plant.

24

Do you ever use a feather duster? Let's take a look at the feather duster worm. Yes, it is a worm. It uses its "feathers" to gather food.

You may have seen bats flying in the night.
But did you know that batfish actually walk?
Yes, they walk on their fins. The top one is a
roughback batfish and the bottom one is
a red-lipped batfish.

Have you ever gone fishing in a pond and caught a sunfish, also called a sunny? If you ever catch an *ocean* sunfish, you will know it! They can grow up to ten feet long and weigh as much as a pickup truck. Can you imagine trying to reel in a fish that big?

Did you imagine frogs looking like this? Well, this is not a frog, but a frogfish. Did you know frogfish go fishing? If you look at the orange one above, you can see its "fishing pole" sticking out in front of its mouth. When a curious little fish comes to look at the lure, "Gulp!" goes the frogfish.

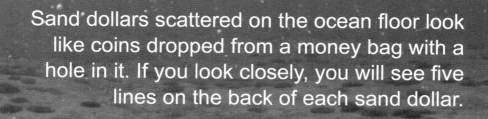

Sand dollars scattered on the ocean floor look like coins dropped from a money bag with a hole in it. If you look closely, you will see five lines on the back of each sand dollar.

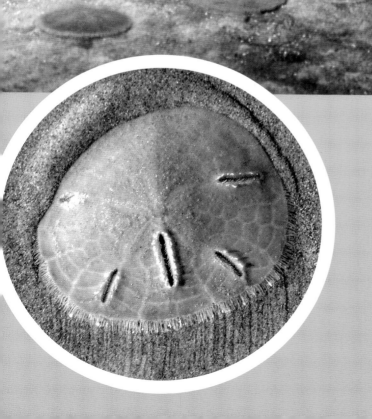

Sand dollars can creep along the ocean floor as they look for food. They like to bury themselves in the sand, like this one.

Look at the beautiful colors of these starfish!
Most starfish have five arms, although some
have more. Like the sea sponge, most starfish
can grow new body parts if they lose them. God
has created more than 1,500 varieties of starfish.

Did someone drop a box of springs out of a boat? No, these blue sea squirts are animals that start out in life looking like tadpoles. They are called sea squirts because they violently squirt water when threatened.

FROG

TAIL   SPIRACLE   EYE   MOUTH

ASCIDIAN

The bottom one is a baby sea squirt. Only God could change that into a blue sea squirt that looks like a spring.

Here is an
octopus!
Octopuses
have eight
arms. Look at
its big, long
head. Do you
see the funnels
that come out
under its eye?

All octopuses have a poisonous bite, but the bite from a blue-ringed octopus (below) can kill an adult human. So don't try to pet an octopus that has blue on it! This one is hiding really well. Can you find its eyes?

A squid is similar to an octopus in that it has eight arms, but it also has two longer tentacles. Most squids are only about two feet long, but one species can grow as long as two pickup trucks!

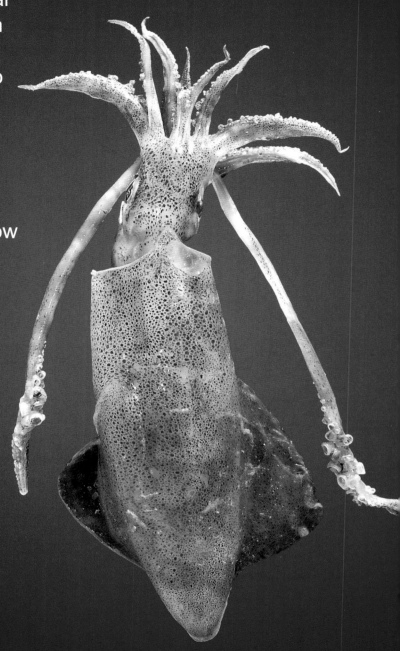

Octopuses are not the only animals in the ocean that can harm people. If you see a Portuguese man o' war lying on the beach like this, do not touch it! The tentacles can give a strong sting. If one is found on a beach, officials may close down the whole beach so no one gets stung.

These animals got the name "man o' war" from sailing warships with the same name. When the man o' war is floating, it uses its top part as a sail to catch the wind, just like a sailboat.

White-spotted jellyfish are beautiful, but swarms of them can deplete the food supply and starve other creatures. That's why it's best for them to stay at home in the western Pacific Ocean where snails prey on them and limit their numbers.

The siphonophore is not a single animal, but several animals hooked together to help each other. None of them could live without the other, and all work together to survive in very deep waters. God wants people to work together like the siphonophore.

You may have heard of ice fishing, but have you ever heard of an icefish? Icefish live in cold water. Some of them live in water almost a mile deep. Although they have blood, it is not red in color. God put something like antifreeze in icefish to keep them from freezing to death.

We saw seahorses earlier. Now let's look at two horseshoe crabs. Notice that many shells are riding piggyback on these horseshoe crabs as they make their way across the sand. This crab got its name from the horseshoe shape of its front end. It uses its tail to turn over if it happens to get flipped onto its back.

This flounder can hide well on the rocky ocean bottom. What is odd about this fish? Look carefully. Both eyes are on the same side of its body! When a flounder is born, its eyes are normal, one on each side of its body. But as it grows, one eye starts moving to the other side. That is so the flounder can lie flat on the bottom of the ocean and still use both of its eyes.

Barnacles are animals that attach themselves to something in the ocean. It may be to a piece of wood or to the body of a whale, as these have done.

Let's look at a few more fish in the sea.

1. The lookdown seems to always be looking down.

2. Triggerfish are often colorful, but they also bite, so be careful!

3. The surgeonfish has a sharp bone like a surgeon's knife near its tail.

We will finish our ocean tour by looking at this bottlenose dolphin. Dolphins are playful creatures. You may see them surfacing in the wake of a boat, like this one. Dolphins "talk" to one another by making clicking sounds, chirps, screams, and whistles.

Well, wasn't that an interesting journey? We can clearly see the power of God in the many wonders He has put in the sea.

Photo credits

About the Author

Mike Atnip, his wife Ellen, and their son Daniel live close to Clark, Ohio. Mike grew up among the cornfields of east-central Indiana, tromping through the fields and woods on a regular basis. Ellen grew up in southeast Pennsylvania, at the foot of Blue Mountain, but later lived in northern New York where the snow piles deep. Daniel was adopted from the tall Andes Mountains in Bolivia, South America, but has spent most of his life in the United States.

The desire of the Atnip family is that people young and old will see God's glory, power, and love in the creation of so many marvelous forms of life and submit their hearts to Him as to a loving Father and Friend.

Mike welcomes reader response and can be contacted at atnips@gmail.com. You may also write to him in care of Christian Aid Ministries, P.O. Box 360, Berlin, Ohio 44610.

Christian Aid Ministries

Christian Aid Ministries was founded in 1981 as a nonprofit, tax-exempt 501(c)(3) organization. Its primary purpose is to provide a trustworthy and efficient channel for Amish, Mennonite, and other conservative Anabaptist groups and individuals to minister to physical and spiritual needs around the world. This is in response to the command ". . . do good unto all men, especially unto them who are of the household of faith" (Galatians 6:10).

Each year, CAM supporters provide approximately 15 million pounds of food, clothing, medicines, seeds, Bibles, Bible story books, and other Christian literature for needy people. Most of the aid goes to orphans and Christian families. Supporters' funds also help to clean up and rebuild for natural disaster victims, put up Gospel billboards in the U.S., support several church-planting efforts, operate two medical clinics, and provide resources for needy families to make their own living. CAM's main purposes for providing aid are to help and encourage God's people and bring the Gospel to a lost and dying world.

CAM has staff, warehouses, and distribution networks in Romania, Moldova, Ukraine, Haiti, Nicaragua, Liberia, and Israel. Aside from management, supervisory personnel, and bookkeeping operations, volunteers do most of the work at CAM locations. Each year, volunteers at our warehouses, field bases, Disaster Response Services projects, and other locations donate over 200,000 hours of work.

CAM's ultimate purpose is to glorify God and help enlarge His kingdom. ". . . whatsoever ye do, do all to the glory of God" (1 Corinthians 10:31).

Creation to Redemption

God created plants, birds, and fish on the first five days. On the sixth day, He created land animals and man. At first man lived in harmony with God and the earth. But after Adam and Eve sinned, some people began to worship the creation rather than the Creator. Others began to selfishly destroy the creation in their pursuit of money, pleasure, or fame.

But God sent His Son Jesus into the world to rescue us from our sin. Jesus taught us to abandon the idolatry of nature worship and to be good stewards of God's creation. He died on the cross and rose again so we could be born again and enter the kingdom of God.

This kingdom of God is made up of those who have allowed Jesus to be King of their lives. Jesus leads these people into a harmonious relationship with God and teaches them to live holy, loving, and unselfish lives as they relate to people and things on this earth. They are in the world but not of the world and look forward to their final redemption in heaven.